Storm & Sky

Serena Craig

BookLeaf Publishing

India | USA | UK

Presentation by *BookLeaf Publishing*

Web: www.bookleafpub.com

E-mail: info@bookleafpub.com

ISBN: 9789357613330

First edition 2023

DEDICATION

To you, for all the countless hours, and to Kimberley Whitcher-Wormald, who first taught me to love birds.

ACKNOWLEDGEMENT

To the custodians of this land on which I stand, my elders past, present and emerging. May we always rise.

PREFACE

There is no specific theme to this little volume, no tight curation. It is simply a collection of my experiences over three weeks of poetic observation. May your souls see mine.

Dog Park Green

Mud spatter,
"On my $300 boots", I idly thought,
Pushing my leather-clad toe, deeper
Into the grass.
Sun blinded, tear-stained and windswept,
Desperate to feel something other than this,
joy on legs bounding before me.
The cockatoos screech their disapproval at such a
mess.
And I breathe in, and out, just like before.

Fuzzy

The edges of the world are blurry today,
Full of wisps I can't catch and words I cannot say.
Too many teeth in my mouth somehow.
My eyes blink slowly against the brightness,
All that blue and green and grey and whiteness,
Too many bells in my brain somehow.
My breath is too loud in my chest today,
Full of wisps I can't catch and words I cannot say.

Salt

Cupped in your hands, the deepest pain of another, and
for one second, you are horrified.
Damp and hot, intimate, foreign,
This salt is not yours,
inescapable,
coating your fingers in its silvery grasp.
I want to remember why I was angry,
I want that feeling to burn and burn and burn me clean, I
need to remember why it mattered so much,
That I mattered so much.
I want to remember that this was mine. Before you took
it from me,
and changed its name.
But now,
Softly you sob, and what leaks from you, leaches from
me, and then, these grief-filled hands, stroke you gently.
I remind you to exhale and live, murmured whispers
hush.
Affirmation.
Absolution.
A love so pure it bursts the walls of my chest.
And I give to you,
what I so desperately want,
Through salt, of my own.

I was born into This

A familiar warble.
Pristine black and white, painted precisely with the
finest edge.
Emerald moss and pungent earth.
Dazzling yellow, clouds of yellow, slashes of yellow,
star-shaped yellow. Was it always this yellow?
Pink, so soft it melts in the breeze,
blushing, bursting, bruised by its graceful descent.
The heavy thrum of mechanical work,
Alien to my ears.
Silence. Whispered leaves.
Coy grass.
That sound again.
A familiar warble.

Je Suis Très Fatigué

I am tired.
Isn't that such a cliche?
I have no clever pattern, no rhyming scheme,
There is nothing profound to say.
But I am tired, and not just today.
Too tired to function
Too tired to eat
The kind of tired that keeps
You awake,
the more you try to sleep.
How can I convey the exhaustion I feel, there are no
words to make this real,
real, even for me.
I am tired today,
with nothing profound to say.

Cafe Jazz

Neon birds,
Strutting in their mechanical gait,
An overflowing fountain,
Useless in so much rain.
We all head for the same shelter, backing away from
the spray,
Nothing music,
Burnt coffee,
A lurid sign that tells us all why we are here.
Some people wear it better than me,
The wind and the rain,
bright pink coat,
trendy boots, is that a beret?
A photo op, against the grey.
A sparrow, real this time,
flits amongst the tables,
making the most of crumbs, among the sodden feet.
Brown patterned wings and beady eyes.
She wears it better than me.

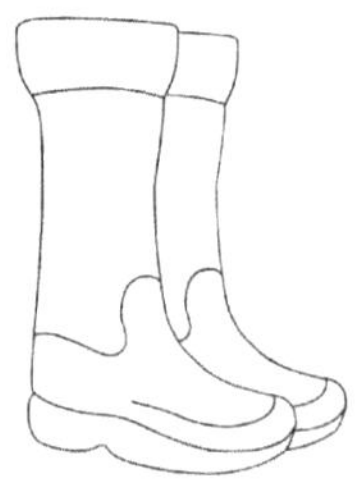

Chill

Flick of a lit cigarette, that acrid blaze,
face on fire with icy cold, eyes narrowed against
razor winds.
Ash dissolves.
Drizzle. More than drizzle. Surely,
that must be rain.
What am I doing here? I never inhale.
Fists deep in olive green cloth, wrapped around my
neck, wool, crowded with scent.
Espresso shots, lavender, Freesias and French
perfume. Earthy herbs.
Smoke.
Me.
You.
What am I doing here?

Mother Earth

Mud spatter,
I cleverly think
On my trendy boots
As my feet sink where the grass once was
"A celebration of sustainability and tiny living"
A quirk in the back of my mind,
As I run my hands over the kitsch.
3D printed plastic snakes.
Rustic macrame coasters.
Artisan candles with industrial names.
$7000 Perspex domes.
$100,000 portable homes,
Just add council taxes, waste disposal and a parking
space,
Soft close fixtures and ambient light,
Bob's your uncle, she'll be right.
In wind-stripped gums and dripping shrubs,
the Galahs snicker at all this mess,
Above
our little eco-fest.

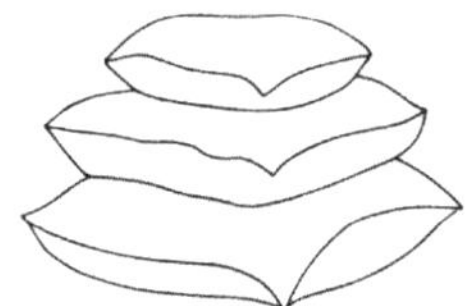

Slip lane

I don't need to be understood to love,
Not really.
My heart is too open for that.
I'll let you poke around the edges of my softness,
knowing you don't know, what you think you know,
or,
At all what that means.
You think you've got it. They always do.
But if you understood, what you think you've got,
Then I wouldn't love you.

Ghosts

I hear you whisper, in silver and green,
Ancient and timeless, your pale limbs delicate,
Yet steadfast.
A canopy of new moons and tiny stars, gentle swirls
in your buttery trunk,
And dimples,
the only signs,
Of the years you have stood your watch.
A study in grace and gravitas,
beauty and strength.
A rustling peace,
an irreverent dance,
The wisdom you have drunk,
From deepest earth,
With roots unseen.

Office (Works)

I work like a doctor
meticulous and clean,
gloved hands, alcohol-soaked pads,
Labeled specimens,
instruments of the trade.
Delicately I remove the plastic shell,
Unclamp the data ribbon,
Each copper shining pin, right where it should have
been, each screw in position.
Nimble fingers undo them all, I get to the guts of the
problem,
sticky flakes
of black and magenta, bleeding into my prepared
disaster zone.
Expertly I stem the flow and heal the wound,
I stitch you back together, neatly.
Perfectly.
Perfectly aligned, each crevice and curve, each
rolling rod clean,
I turn you gently on
And get the same,
Error screen.

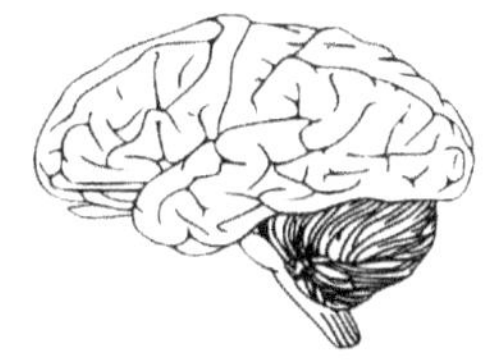

Fifteen Months

You handed me your crackers,
as you wandered away,
waving briefly,
not much to say.

Distracted by the Raven,
Noisy above your head,
watching closely,
Softly you tread.

Kangaroo in the bushes,
As you wander away,
Stepping lightly,
Not much to say.

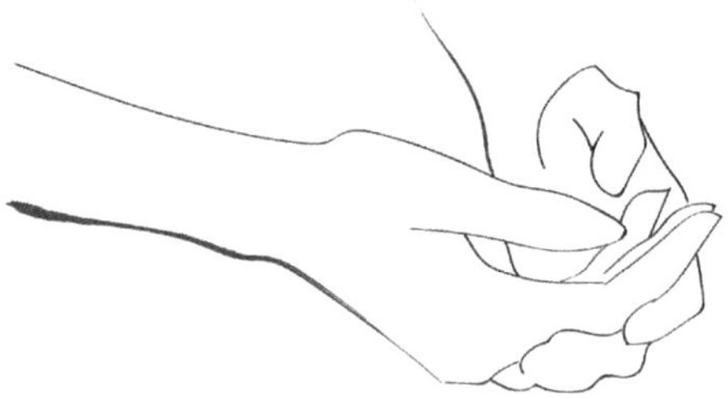

Brown Eyed Boy

Light streams through your honeyed gaze,
And with one good look, you dissolve me.
Caramel and chestnut and chocolate satin,
your Lion eyes,
see right through me.
There is no greater warmth than
The gold in every glance,
the blazing sun captured,
In pools of ancient depth.
I could bathe in that stare,
eternally
Content in the heat,
Of your forever love.

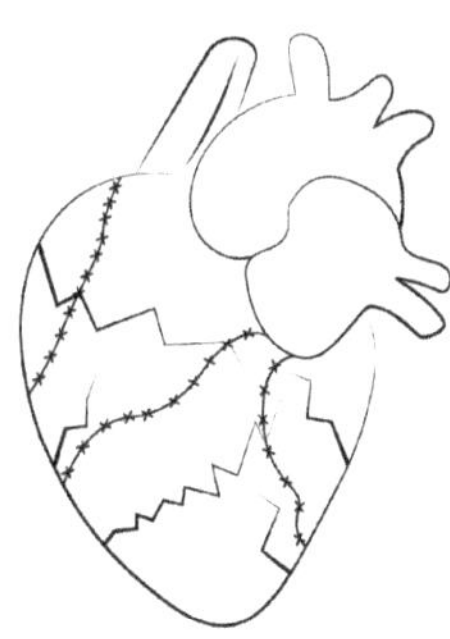

Emergency

"Collect all fragments from the area,
And meet at the assemblage point,"
the command of the speaker,
the rules of the game.
"I'm from Coma quadrant."
"And what about you?"
"I got my first piece in Trauma"
Small smile,
Nothing special,
Nothing new.
We carry our bags,
on our silent way,
a thronging crowd of thousands,
looking for pay.
"Collect all fragments from the area
and meet at the assemblage point."
The speaker commands.
We know it by heart,
day in day out,
Doing our part.
"For king and for country"
We carry the metal,
rusted and sharp,
a gathering of thousands,
Looking for hearth,
and home
and heart.

Dicksonia Antarcticus

Serenely you unfurl
Reaching out,
From deep inside your perfect curl
Unsteady, but roots firm
Your leaves begin marching,
Turn by turn,
Up,
Ever up to the sun.
DNA of sacred geometry
perfect choreography
Tender and newly green,
Waiting,
Waiting to be seen.

Fear and Feathers

I buried a bird today,
So damaged I couldn't tell,
what sort she was.
Unexpected, my tears slid,
Into the earth, as I lay red berries, white flowers and
leafy greens,
over this impromptu grave.
May your wings forever beat,
in pristine skies,
above the soil,
That lies beneath our feet

The Golden Arches

So many Crows here,
Glossy and fat,
Or maybe they're ravens.
Never got the
hang of
That,
Seeing the difference, between two birds,
Superbly black.
They pick through the garbage,
expertly slack,
Fine dining,
Amongst the
Crap.
A double quarter pounder,
Do you want fries with that?
Nahh, they say,
In that way that they do,
Happy with what's there,
Entirely aware,
Of the metal spikes,
Designed only,
To keep out the
Likes,
Of them.

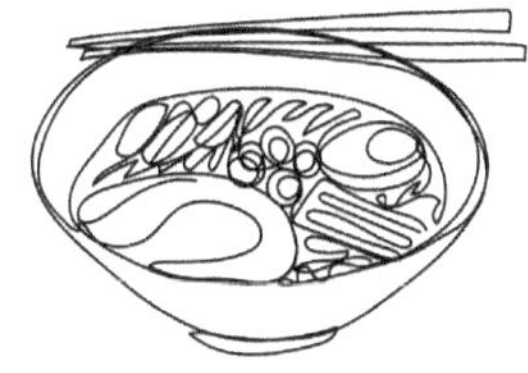

The Void has a Heart

It exploded,
From within the depths of purple and blue,
of Indigo, and gentle magenta.
Bright, and golden, orange with fury around its
edges, a ceaseless hurtling.
Almond shaped, forcing itself into the darkened orb,
with nothing but the need to permeate,
contact is made.
Let there be light.
She is knocked back,
Bruised and concave, limbs and hair forming a
terrible arc,
tendrils,
seaweed strands, strips of a white flag,
shredded by the blast.
No surrender here.
No ribs where there should be,
Only light.
No flesh where it should be,
Only light.
No soft skin where it should be,
Only light.
No pain where it should be.
Only light.

Where the River Bends

Blistering heat from
dusty gravel,
Thick air,
even the ancient gums
cannot stand it
anymore.
They stand stoically,
with cracking bark and
tinderbox leaves,
waiting for a reprieve.
I stumble down the
well-worn track,
with eyes for nothing
else,
But that first generous
stretch of welcome
brown,
Flowing ever, ever
down.
A little further, over
bone dry boards,
I don't even take off
my dress,
Find the rocks that
mark my way,
My $2 Kmart shoes,
worth every single
step,
As I find relief, calf
deep.
Unsteady,

lurch forward,
I break the long-held
tension,
as she brings me into
her embrace.
Cool and chaotic,
fabric and hair, I'm
gratified I don't
audibly sizzle.
I am home, in a current
centuries older than I,
and here,
Here I shed it all.
Nothing more euphoric
than this.
Nothing more
cleansing than this.
Nothing more peaceful
than this.
It is here, I truly exist.

Who Owns the Flowers Anyway?

Soft hands that gently steal,
A stem, a stalk, a single branch.
They smell like honey and salt and heat,
They look like joy and cartwheels on sand,
and sing of warm nights and inky skies,
textures of paper, miniature needles, puffs of light,
Soft like a cat,
Scents and memories,
Caught in the act.

Rumble Strip

A footy jersey and a 6 pack of VB,
White rose wreath,
On polished Oak,
As you lay in the back of a black
2 door,
Ford Fairlane.
We did 100 down the Highway,
You, me and Anubis,
entrusted with the last,
of your earthly journey.
He wore a suit, with the windows rolled down,
his eyes disguised,
Gold Aviators.
I listened to Kanye West,
with my window rolled down,
wishing I'd somehow known,
Wishing I'd somehow chosen,
something more reverent,
for our processional.
But maybe it was perfect,
a tinny,
under that brilliant sun,
and maybe you'd have smiled,
as we passed your final mile.

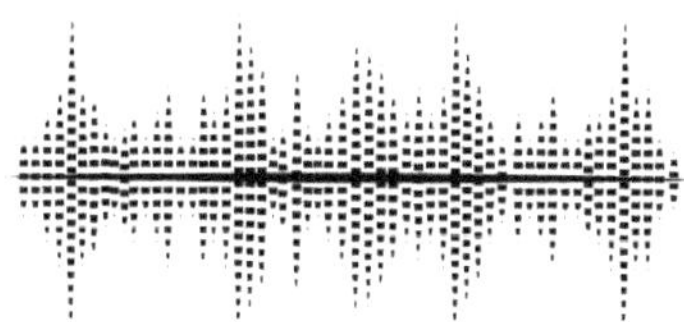